I want to thank my family for
giving me love in ways that are hard for others to understand.
I want to thank my grandparents for
helping raise me when people stepped out of the picture.
I want to thank my aunts and uncles for always being there to make me laugh.
And especially my mom and sister for
being there for me when I couldn't hold myself up.

I thought it was normal
to wake up to
screaming
in the middle of the night.
That it was normal to wear earplugs
and act like it was just the TV.
That the yelling was just the
neighbor's... until I grew up and
realized.
No.
That isn't "normal".

I sit in my bed with my fingers crossed
that you don't come in.
Please don't yell.
Please don't make me come out.
Please.
I pray.
Hoping that it passes 2AM...
with no footsteps.
No questions.
No phone searching.
And no cleaning.

My teacher took my phone.
She wondered...
why in the world
does an 8 year old have this?
It's better to let her wonder
than to know the truth...
To know that I am forced
to spy
on my parents.
That I am forced to tell.
If I don't
I get...

              well, you'll see later.

The car door slams.
Garage door shakes.
Doors rattle.
Drunk.
here it comes.
The one thing that gives me the most anxiety.
Where my anxiety
comes from.
I can't let him know I'm scared.
He gets a rise out of making
me
upset.
WHO WAS HERE?
WHO WAS THAT CAR?
What...
what car...
no car was here.
NO.
YOU'RE GROUNDED.
smack

I am told to *polish*.
Faster.
Better.
Make it clean.
Scrub.
Scrub the stove.
Clean the oven.
            Wipe the counters.

        DONT.
        DO NOT.

ASK QUESTIONS.
I don't know why he's so anal.
Why?
Doesn't matter.
Just do it.
            If only the little girl knew she was helping him cover up.

We sat in the cold.
After running out of my *home*.
We sat on my friend's steps.
Phone in hand.
Calling *911*.
Moms *shadow* in the window.
Screams in the distance.
Blue lights.
It's okay...
I promise
we will be
Okay.

Why are you always asleep?
Why are there so many mirrors?
Why are so many random people always coming
here? Don't ask why.
You don't want to know.
What you don't know...
won't hurt you...
well...
Kinda

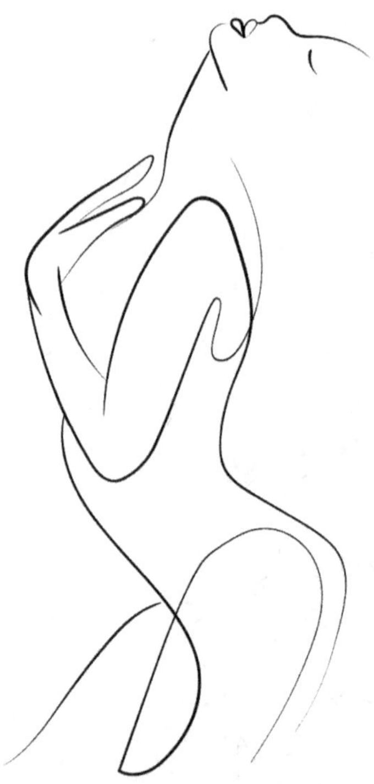

The scars on my arms are from me.
Yet are because of haunting memories.
Failure.
Let down.
Anxiety.
Abuse.
Neglect.
It isn't a normal life.
It's beyond complicated.
Poverty vs Rich.
Abuse vs Mental Neglect.
Love vs Care.
Family. VS. F A M I L Y.
Blood vs Heart.
Which is me?
I don't know.

Why does treat her differently?

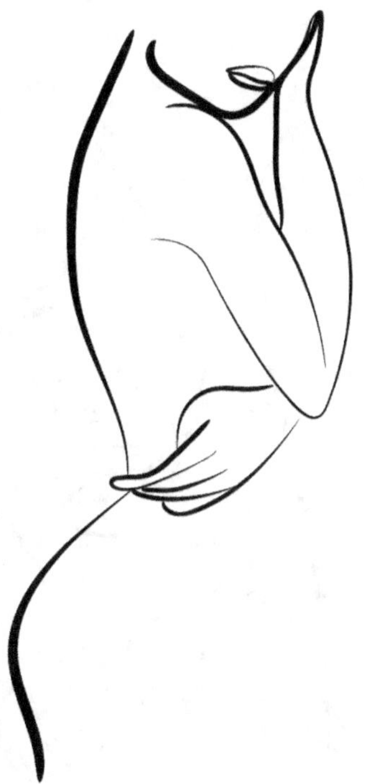

He would never lay his hands on her.
Tell her she is a waste of space.
A bitch.
The worst person he's ever met.
Problem causer.
He would never even think

about doing or saying any
of the things he does to me.
He would never lock the windows
to smoke.
Would never smack her
because she had to do homework instead of cleaning.
Tell her to
starve herself.
Why me?

Growing up.
Alone.
Realizing you aren't... them.
Why,
Why did you leave?
Why,
Why are people telling me to reach
out? What,
What actually happened?

Now you are gone.
And you are gone.
And all of the answers are gone.

Now   I   really
am, alone.

But mommy, why?
Why I cry?
Why I cry to you?
Asking why?
Why is there glass in the car?
Why is there another car to drive?
My car seat mom...
Please?
Why mommy.
Enough.
Please don't hide. I don't want to have to record why.

The stranger.
He picks me up.
Yet this stranger has been around longer than the last.

I get asked,
Where, who, and what is he doing.
If I don't respond like you ask...
I get grounded.
Then I can't see mommy.

A new stranger.
He picks me up.
Yet we drive fast.
He scares me.
He drinks too.
Loud music when I try to sleep.
Yells and screams while I try to eat.
Bangs and crashes while I count the sheep.

    Why mommy.
    Why?

New stranger.
Dads mad.
Breaks windows.
Comes over.

Yet,
I am told.
PICK.
Who do I pick?

      Neither.

Christmas Night.
What a fight.
Yelling and screaming all night.

It's okay sis.
He will be here soon.
Just listen for reindeer on the roof.

Christmas Night.
What a fight.
Smacking and pushing all night.

It's almost time.
Stay asleep.
I'll see if he has come in your sleep.

Christmas Night.
What a fight.

He didn't come at all last night.

It's   okay.
I'll set up.

Please. Please. Don't get up.

Playing in the snow.
All I want is to go.
I just want a normal day with no yelling,
Screaming,
Fighting,
Pushing.

My teacher says,
Stay outside.
Hunny,
Hide.
But I'm worried about
mom. What about the
family?
What about my sister?
Nana?
What should I do?
How do I live like this?

Daddy and Mommy won't stop fighting.

3 ply toilet paper
Coffee filters

Too warm
Too cold

love
LOVE

Shopping
DIY

Full fridge
Spoons of peanut butter
Name brand
Store brand

I love both. Both are very different.
Both created me.

Someone's trying their best.
To never judge,
To never question,

You never know.

How low it can go.

Abuse:
I hope I don't follow the same footsteps.
I hope I don't follow the same footsteps.
I hope I don't follow the same footsteps.

Success:
I hope I do follow the same footsteps.
I hope I do follow the same footsteps.
I hope I do follow the same footsteps.

Family:
I hope
I hope
I hope

Love:
I hope it is healthy
Please.
I can't take the memories.
I hope it is healthy
Please.
I can't take the memories.
I hope it is healthy
Please.
I can't take the memories.

Someone once told me,
Family isn't blood.
It is how you love.

If family isn't always blood.
And is from love...
                    Why did you "take" me into yours?
You don't love me.
You only like the idea of me.

My real family is the ones who endlessly love me. Papa. Yaya. Mom.

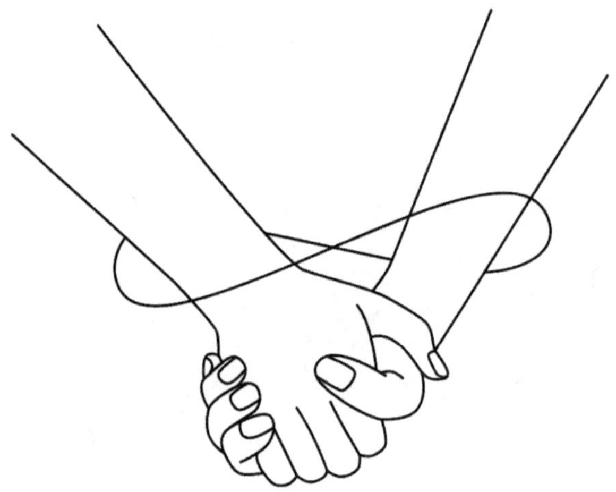

The idea of me,
To you,
Is like a bragging point.

The confidence booster that you took me.
But in reality,
The family that raised me.

Is your parents.

You didn't dad the way a dad is supposed to.

And that hurts.

Why does it hurt so bad?
Why do I compare myself to her?
Why do I think I'm not worthy of love.
Why did I strike out 2x.
All I have been told is...
I love you.
I have been shown.
I hate you.

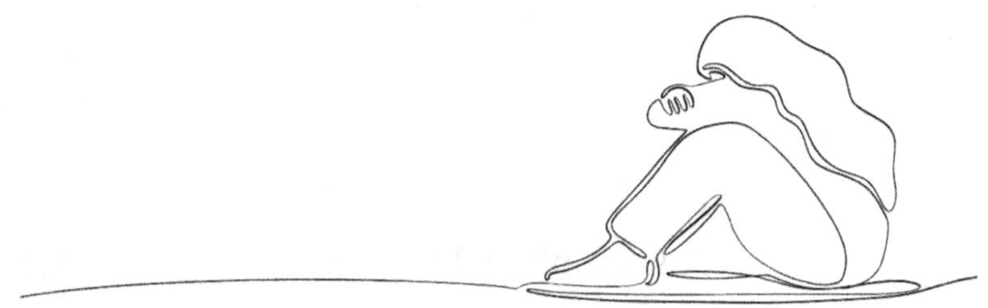

Please God,
I pray I heal.
I pray I know I will be okay.

To those of you,
who struggle with mental illness.
Who constantly wish
there was a back button.
This is for you.

I didn't ask.
I didn't ask to be hit.
I didn't ask to be broken.

Why did you scream at me? Why did you smack me?
It's okay...
It'll get better.

I didn't ask to be loved.
I just hoped.
I didn't beg you to answer me. I didn't ask to be cheated on..
Why did you go?
Why did you go?
Please. Stay.